HOLIDAY HISTORY
DAY OF THE DEAD

by Claudia Oviedo

pogo

Ideas for Parents and Teachers

Pogo Books let children practice reading informational text while introducing them to nonfiction features such as headings, labels, sidebars, maps, and diagrams, as well as a table of contents, glossary, and index.

Carefully leveled text with a strong photo match offers early fluent readers the support they need to succeed.

Before Reading

- "Walk" through the book and point out the various nonfiction features. Ask the student what purpose each feature serves.
- Look at the glossary together. Read and discuss the words.

Read the Book

- Have the child read the book independently.
- Invite him or her to list questions that arise from reading.

After Reading

- Discuss the child's questions. Talk about how he or she might find answers to those questions.
- Prompt the child to think more. Ask: Day of the Dead celebrates and honors people who have died. How do you celebrate and honor loved ones who have died?

Pogo Books are published by Jump!
5357 Penn Avenue South
Minneapolis, MN 55419
www.jumplibrary.com

Copyright © 2023 Jump! International copyright reserved in all countries. No part of this book may be reproduced in any form without written permission from the publisher.

Library of Congress Cataloging-in-Publication Data

Names: Oviedo, Claudia, author.
Title: Day of the dead / by Claudia Oviedo.
Description: Minneapolis: Jump!, Inc., [2023]
Series: Holiday history | Includes index.
Audience: Ages 7-10
Identifiers: LCCN 2022024435 (print)
LCCN 2022024436 (ebook)
ISBN 9798885241229 (hardcover)
ISBN 9798885241236 (paperback)
ISBN 9798885241243 (ebook)
Subjects: LCSH: All Soul's Day—Juvenile literature.
Mexico—Social life and customs—Juvenile literature.
Classification: LCC GT4995.A4 O95 2023 (print)
LCC GT4995.A4 (ebook)
DDC 394.266—dc23
LC record available at https://lccn.loc.gov/2022024435
LC ebook record available at https://lccn.loc.gov/2022024436

Editor: Eliza Leahy
Designer: Molly Ballanger

Photo Credits: Shutterstock, cover, 23; Fernando Macias Romo/iStock, 1; Pixel-Shot/Shutterstock, 3; Birol Bali/Shutterstock, 4; lunamarina/Shutterstock, 5; Matyas Rehak/Shutterstock, 6-7; Richard Ellis/Alamy, 8-9; Shandor/Shutterstock, 10; JannHuizenga/iStock, 11; Litvalifa/Shutterstock, 12; Valerie Loiseleux/iStock, 12-13; Brphoto/Dreamstime, 14-15; Dina Julayeva/Shutterstock, 16; Paul Aiken/Digital First Media/Boulder Daily Camera/Getty, 17; Lucy.Brown/Shutterstock, 18-19; Eve Orea/Shutterstock, 20-21.

Printed in the United States of America at Corporate Graphics in North Mankato, Minnesota.

TABLE OF CONTENTS

CHAPTER 1
Celebrating the Dead................................4

CHAPTER 2
Day of the Dead Traditions....................10

CHAPTER 3
Day of the Dead Around the World.........16

QUICK FACTS & TOOLS
Day of the Dead Place of Origin............22
Quick Facts..22
Glossary...23
Index...24
To Learn More.......................................24

CHAPTER 1
CELEBRATING THE DEAD

Thousands of years ago, many people lived in what is now Mexico. The Aztecs were one group who lived here. Tenochtitlán was the center of their **empire**.

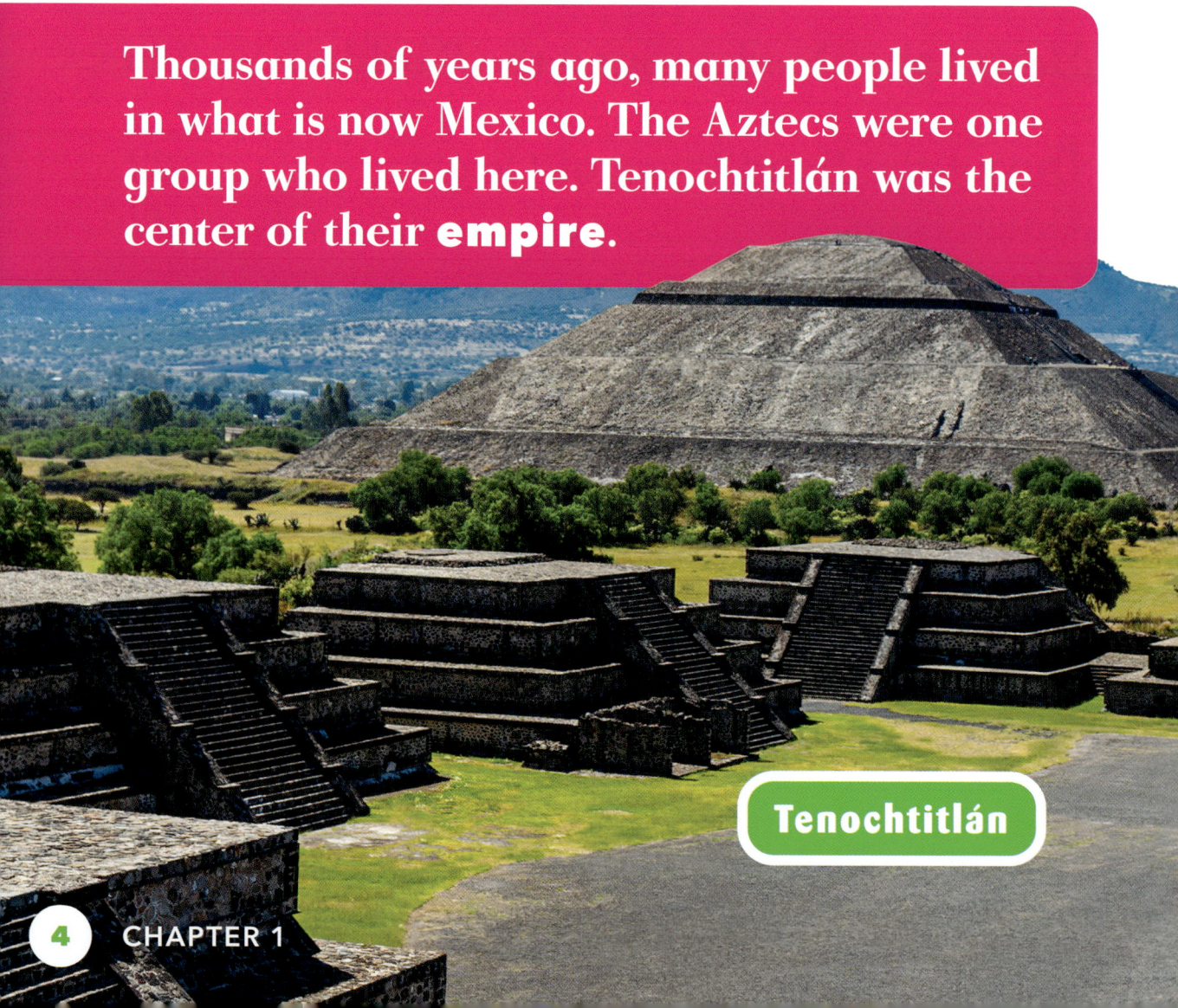

Tenochtitlán

The Aztecs believed death was part of the **cycle** of life. They celebrated it. Skulls were **symbols** of death. They put out food, water, and tools for the dead. Why? They believed these helped **souls** on their journey to the Land of the Dead. This was their final resting place.

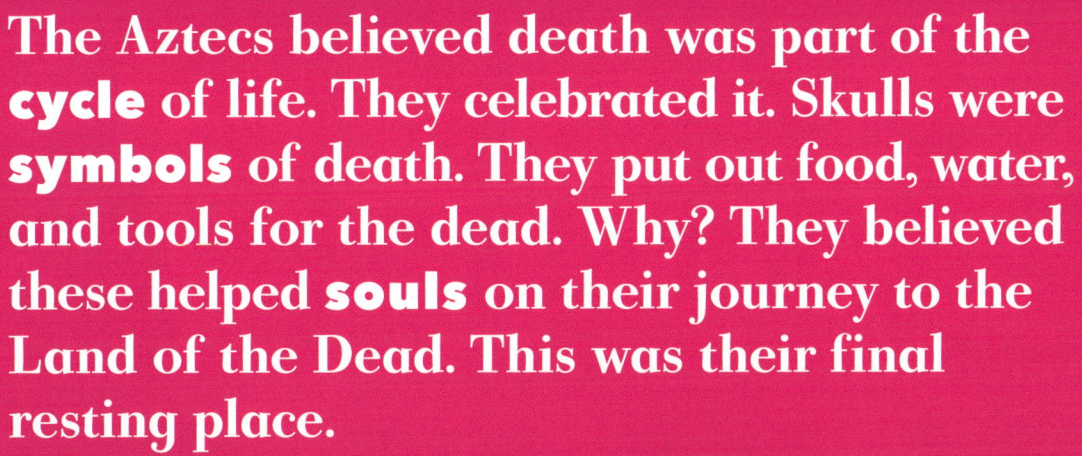

skull

At this time, many people in Spain were **Catholic**. On November 1, they celebrated **saints** on All Saints' Day. On November 2, they celebrated the dead on All Souls' Day. They visited graves. People brought drinks, bread, flowers, and candles.

In the 1500s, Spanish **conquerors** came to Mexico. Catholic and Aztec **traditions** mixed. This is how Day of the Dead formed.

This holiday is celebrated on November 1 and 2. Families and friends gather. They invite the souls of loved ones who have died to visit the Land of the Living. It is a celebration!

WHAT DO YOU THINK?

Day of the Dead combines traditions from different **cultures**. What traditions do you practice? Do you know what cultures they come from?

CHAPTER 1   9

CHAPTER 2
DAY OF THE DEAD TRADITIONS

Day of the Dead is a colorful holiday. Yellow, orange, red, purple, pink, white, and black are common. Skulls are still an important symbol. People decorate sugar skulls. They are made from sugar.

sugar skulls

Skeletons are another common symbol. The most famous is La Catrina. She wears a fancy hat. People dress up like her for parades and festivals.

People decorate with papel picado. These paper banners are colorful. They have detailed patterns. People hang them at festivals and other celebrations. They also place them on **altars**.

DID YOU KNOW?

Marigolds are another symbol of this holiday. The smell helps souls find their way back to the Land of the Living. People also make these flowers out of paper.

marigold

CHAPTER 2

papel picado

CHAPTER 2

altar

People visit cemeteries. They tell stories. They clean up graves. They set up altars in cemeteries or at home. They place **offerings** on the altars.

14 CHAPTER 2

TAKE A LOOK!

What are some common altar offerings? Take a look!

belongings
such as toys, books, photos, or other items of importance to the dead

calaveras de azúcar
decorated sugar skulls

candles
to light the way for souls

cempasúchiles
marigolds

favorite meals
to feed the souls

pan de muerto
bread decorated with dried fruit and colored sugar

papel picado
colorful paper cut into fancy patterns

water
to give souls something to drink

CHAPTER 2

CHAPTER 3
DAY OF THE DEAD AROUND THE WORLD

Day of the Dead is celebrated in many places. In Mexico, people celebrate at home. They also celebrate in cemeteries with music and dancing. Some cities have festivals or parades.

In the United States, some communities and schools celebrate. People set up altars. Kids learn how to cut papel picado. Others decorate sugar skulls.

CHAPTER 3
17

Celebrations around the world honor the dead on November 2. In Guatemala, people fly big kites. Why? These are thought to scare away bad spirits.

In El Salvador, people dress up as characters from **myths**.

CHAPTER 3 19

Day of the Dead is more popular than ever. People gather. They honor the dead. They enjoy colorful flowers, sugar skulls, and food. They watch skeletons dance in parades. Do you celebrate Day of the Dead? If not, would you like to?

WHAT DO YOU THINK?

Day of the Dead honors and celebrates people who have died. Do you think this is important? Why or why not?

CHAPTER 3

CHAPTER 3

QUICK FACTS & TOOLS

DAY OF THE DEAD PLACE OF ORIGIN

QUICK FACTS

Dates: November 1 and 2

Time of Origin: 3,000 years ago

Place of Origin: Aztec Empire, Mexico

Common Symbols: candles, papel picado, marigolds, sugar skulls, skeletons

Foods: favorite meals or foods of the dead, pan de muerto

Traditions: setting up altars, visiting cemeteries and graves, eating special bread, decorating sugar skulls, going to community celebrations

GLOSSARY

altars: Places to put offerings for people who have died.

Catholic: Of or relating to the branch of Christianity that accepts the Pope as its leader.

conquerors: People who gain something by force.

cultures: Ideas, customs, traditions, and ways of life of certain groups of people.

cycle: A series of events that repeats in the same order.

empire: A group of countries or states that has the same ruler.

myths: Old stories that express the beliefs or history of a group of people or explain natural events.

offerings: Items left out for the souls of people who have died.

saints: In certain Christian churches, people who have been officially recognized for having lived very holy lives.

souls: The spiritual parts of people that are believed to give life to bodies.

symbols: Objects or designs that stand for, suggest, or represent something else.

traditions: Customs, ideas, or beliefs that are handed down from one generation to the next.

INDEX

All Saints' Day 6
All Souls' Day 6
altars 12, 14, 15, 17
Aztecs 4, 5, 9
death 5, 9, 20
El Salvador 19
festivals 11, 12, 16
graves 6, 14
Guatemala 19
La Catrina 11
Land of the Dead 5
Land of the Living 9, 12
marigolds 12, 15
Mexico 4, 9, 16
offerings 14, 15
papel picado 12, 15, 17
parades 11, 16, 20
skeletons 11, 20
skulls 5, 10
souls 5, 6, 9, 12, 15
Spain 6
sugar skulls 10, 15, 17, 20
Tenochtitlán 4
United States 17

TO LEARN MORE

Finding more information is as easy as 1, 2, 3.
1. Go to www.factsurfer.com
2. Enter "DayoftheDead" into the search box.
3. Choose your book to see a list of websites.